GOD IS AN ANARCHIST

Cam Rea

With Foreword by Gary Chartier

Table of Contents

ACKNOWLEDGMENTS

I would like to thank the reader first. Whether you enjoy the book or not, I appreciate that you took the time to consider the idea presented.

The concept of this book goes back more than a decade ago. The idea first came to me during a sermon on the book of Judges back in 1996 when I attained a small church in the city of Walkerton, Indiana. I spent many years at this church and will never forget the great conversations and the wonderful people who attended every Sabbath. Therefore, I would like thank all of them for their input and ideas.

I collected many notes over the years and decided to take those notes and turn it into a book. I started this project late last year and finished in late spring. I was not sure to whom I should present this manuscript, but then I came across Gary Chartier, who currently serves as Professor of Law and Business Ethics and Associate Dean of the Tom and Vi Zapara School of Business at La Sierra University in Riverside, California. I asked Gary Chartier if he would be interested in reading it over and, if he liked, providing a foreword for the book. He accepted and read over the manuscript, providing further insight that was beneficial. Thank you, Gary.

I also want to send a big thank you to Janice Sue Shepherd for taking the time and working with me in editing this book. Without Janice's help, I would be months behind. Once again, thank you, Janice!

Next, I want to thank Jeffrey Tucker, the Executive Editor of Laissez-Faire Books. If anyone can critique a book and tell you its value, Mr. Tucker is the man to do so. When I first sent the work to him for further review, I was nervous. However, my nerves were calmed when I got his message later on. He was thrilled with the work and the promising future it holds. Thank you for taking the time and providing much needed advice.

Also, I would like to thank the author Tarrin Lupo, along with Reagen Dandridge Desilets, for their advice on eBook publishing, and I want to thank my good friend Brett Schlotterback for helping me keep the computer running.

Lastly, I would like to thank my family. I want to thank my parents for their endless support and encouragement. But, the biggest thank you goes to my wife and two sons for putting up with my odd hours and coffee drinking.

Foreword

by Gary Chartier

Anarchists frequently view religion as exemplifying or sustaining arbitrary authority. Consider Mikhail Bakunin's *God and the State*, suggesting that subservience to the state is disturbingly similar to religious belief, and Daniel Guerin's *No Gods, No Masters*, effectively treating religious and socio-political authority as coordinate.

When religious institutions are intertwined with a society's power structure, just as when those institutions reinforce submissiveness to authority by denigrating or otherwise resisting critical thinking, it's easy to see why they might be seen as anarchism's enemies. But it is also surely crucial to recognize alternative strands in the history of multiple religious traditions. In the Abrahamic traditions, which I know best, it is clear, for instance, that belief in divine transcendence has undermined the idolization of political authority; that belief in individual access to God and to divine truth has strengthened belief in the capacity of ordinary people to make their own political decisions; and that Jesus' praise of peace has inspired rejection of state-made wars and the search for a truly consensual society. Religion and authoritarianism may sometimes be allies, but the story is too mixed to make it reasonable to insist that they have to be.

Cam Rea's *God is an Anarchist* is an attempt to explore the anti-authoritarian side of Christianity. It is structured primarily as a reading of the Bible, with a focus on biblical passages that might be thought to lend support to the state's putative legitimacy, as well as on those that can be seen as counting against it.

Rea sees humans as created co-creators endowed by God with a freedom their creator intends for them to use, not abandon. He suggests readings of the Ten Commandments, not as arbitrary impositions, but rather as sources of freedom. The familiar story of the Tower of Babel should be read, he maintains, as a divine condemnation of centralized political authority. The prophet Samuel's warning, and the events following it, highlight the fact that kingship was bad for Israel, just as being ruled is bad for people today.

The establishment of a system of tithes described in the Hebrew Bible does not, Rea argues, justify the collection of taxes by the state (or the treatment of contributions to the church as morally or spiritually required). Neither Jesus nor St. Paul, he believes, can be read as having identified the payment of taxes as a moral duty.

While Rea urges support for the plausible view that the use of force to defend oneself or others against unjust attack is appropriate, he amasses support for the view that the God of the Bible hates war (he takes the opportunity to emphasize that the Bible provides no support for conscription or the maintenance of a standing army—both

VI

obviously tools of repression and aggression). Ultimately, God rules, and seeks to rule, by empowering, not by dominating: God does not want to be an autocrat or to underwrite the autocratic rule of any human person or institution.

Rea's theological and exegetical proposals should prompt thoughtful conversation among proponents of biblical authority. But they should also serve as food for thought for more liberal Christians, as well as for anarchists and other anti-authoritarians who assume that the only way to read the Bible and the Christian tradition is as supporting vigorous social and political authority. I encourage readers, whatever their views, to ask themselves what they might be able to learn from Rea's thoughtful reading of the Bible through anarchist eyes.

—GARY CHARTIER
Center for a Stateless Society
June 3, 2012

Introduction

What is God? Many Christians and Jews I have talked with concerning the makeup of God over the years say he is the creator and ruler of the universe, a moral authority for man to live by and, in essence, the Supreme Being. Of course, this depends on the person with whom you are talking. The atheist will answer that there is no God. From those who believe in a God, but have no affiliation with religion, you will get a mixed multitude of answers. Some view God as a living tyrant who cares little of what is happening on Earth but pays attention and seems apathetic. Others take the deist approach, suggesting God took off after creating the Earth, leaving it to the natural laws; thus, leaving mankind to a fate uncertain but natural. There are many other views, of course, besides what you have read.

The focus of this book does not support some sort of established denominational dogmatic view of God, but rather those who have belief in God or maybe no belief. The point this book looks to make is that God, whether real or mythical, does not favor a religion or a denomination of a certain branch professing to believe. The book you're about to read will demonstrate that God could care less about the building or the dogma that is spewed forth from the pulpit every Sabbath, Sunday, or any other day of the week.

This book will also demonstrate that God could care less about a state, kingdom, or empire. God does not favor politics. Yes, God may love the fact that some politicians try to restore faith in him through political means and actions, but what principle can we find to base that this is what God wanted or willed?

In essence, one must be careful in trying to determine what God favors in both church and politics. It has become all too common throughout the course of human history, where politicians use churches and churches use politicians to establish some sort of principle that God would favor. This is due to those seeking power through ignorance by invoking God's name to gain the vote, the will, and the obedience of the masses. God detests coercive power for it favors not liberty, nor allows the individual to thrive. Coercive power is used to blanket the eyes of humanity, which in turn leads to further suffering in many forms both physical and emotional. This is the unfortunate aspect, even though many politicians and ministers do believe they are doing the right thing, they all fail. Some ministers forecast endlessly that the end of America or the world is soon, praying that humanity will turn its heart back to God in order to avoid such circumstances. The ministers who spread this fear are religious statist. These ministers do not want the state to end, but rather the state to embrace their God and vice versa.

Therefore, ministers and politicians who embrace the state and all its frauds will use and abuse God when it is convenient. God is but a vehicle, rented as a means to get what they want by evoking his name. They do so to gain a vote by spreading fear to fill both the religious and political pews.

In my research into what does God really believe, as opposed to what we think he believes, I conclude that God does not agree with an establishment of religion or a political body, but God is rather a being of principle that favors all, so long as the people are allowed to live as individuals without coercion and government. This, however, does not mean God favors sin, but one also should remember that God does not hate the sinner.

Chapter 1

God: That Great Central Planner

In the beginning God created the heaven and the earth.
—Genesis 1:1.

Is God a central planner? Over the years the question has arisen whether or not God is indeed a central planner. Most religious people of various faiths will say yes, God had a central plan that he used to create the universe. Others, who are atheists or agnostic, will say the same thing but in the negative sense. They equate God as being no different from the state due to central planning.

The difference between the two is that one group says it is good, while the other group will say it is bad. This is based on the concept of the state. The state is indeed a central planner, a forcible illusion by which all of society is live and thrive. Almost every "ism" connected to the idea of the state throughout history, has used the name of God to invoke the state's will upon the people by divine right. This is bad. I agree with those who say that central planning is bad and just plain wrong, for it inhibits the individual from moving forward. On the other hand, central planning is not totally bad so long as it is left up to individuals to plan their missions, projects, and lives.

Now, back to our question of is God a central planner? The answer is yes and no. According to the Bible, God had a plan to create; we read of this in the first chapter of the book of Genesis. This creation is everything we see before us, the air we breathe, the land we walk on, the water we swim in, and Mankind must provide proper care for this property given to him freely. Mankind is an extension of his plan, a physical representation of God himself. In essence, man is a demigod waiting to be like God. God was a central planner for only a brief moment; when his work was finished, his living canvas had domain over his work, free of charge.

Chapter 2

The Tree of Free Will

The Garden of Eden, according to most religious people among the Judeo-Christian belief, is the birthplace of humanity. To others, it is a mythological tale with some relevance. To most, it is an intriguing tale, whether they believe it or not.

Nevertheless, what is interesting and unique among the religious community concerning the Garden of Eden, is found to be rather odd among many individuals of no secular faith, that a tree was the deciding factor between the relationship of God and man. The book of Genesis 1:11-12 states:

> Then God said, "Let the earth bring forth grass, the herb that yields seed, and the fruit tree that yields fruit according to its kind, whose seed is in itself, on the earth"; and it was so. And the earth brought forth grass, the herb that yields seed according to its kind, and the tree that yields fruit, whose seed is in itself according to its kind. And God saw that it was good.[1]

---

[1] New King James Version, as elsewhere unless noted otherwise.

The tree that produces fruit is a symbol of life, a symbol of production, a symbol that it reproduces fruit after its own kind after its own system. But, one tree stood alone.

> And the Lord God commanded the man, saying, "Of every tree of the garden you may freely eat; but of the tree of the knowledge of good and evil you shall not eat, for in the day that you eat of it you shall surely die."[2]

God's message is simple, you eat and you die. God is not saying mankind cannot eat from the "tree of the knowledge," but rather warning of the consequences if they do so. If Adam and Eve eat from the tree, they will still be alive, but they cannot stay in Eden. Eden is an artificial heaven and God cannot allow them to stay, for God cannot dwell in sin. Even the tree God told Adam and Eve not to eat from is not sinful, but rather an extension of God's belief in choice. Satan had his way, telling Eve, "For God knows that in the day you eat of it your eyes will be opened, and you will be like God, knowing good and evil."[3] Adam and Eve were curious of course and ate from the forbidden tree. Their eyes did not open in some mystical sense, but rather guilt set in because they were told not to eat from the tree.

---

[2] Genesis 2:16-17.
[3] Genesis 3:5.

Had Adam and Eve refrained from eating the forbidden tree, they would have lived a long life, only to leave their physical body for an immortal one; there is no death in the realm of God. Since they ate from the forbidden tree, although they were physically and spiritually connected to God, they could not transform into spirit and become like God when they died. Instead, they have to wait for his return, just as we do today.[4]

Some may find this as a sick game between God and Satan to see who wins the bet. But it's not a game, rather it is free will. God is not a dictator, for if he is why did he allow Satan to rebel so easily? God hoped that his children would not eat of the fruit. People may ask why did God place the tree there if he knew what could happen. No matter how hard one protects their children, one still has to allow for choice. Of course, God hoped his children would make the right choice, but he will not hold their hand in the process. As parents, we protect our children, but realize they must make choices that are best for them and for them alone. Sometimes they make the right choice and sometimes they make the wrong choice, but that is life and that is learning.

In summary, God believes in free will and the Eden story backs this. Adam and Eve chose their path the same as we choose our path. God hoped Adam and Eve would choose and live in his system of liberty and they still did, or at least partially, even after they were banished from Eden. They were living no more in the land of luxury and

---

[4] See Romans 5:12; 1 Corinthians 15:21.

Godology. They still had free will and choice in the wild, but the wild provided no luxury as Eden had. Because of this loss in luxury and abundance, their children and the descendants of those children must decide to live in liberty or statism. Unfortunately, today, we live among those who chose statism as the path towards enlightenment.

Chapter 3

Those Ten Commandments

The Ten Commandments are found in the books of Exodus and Deuteronomy, also known as the "Ten Utterances" or the "Ten Sayings." These commandments were set in two tablets of stone, given to Moses at Mount Sinai. These commandments are from the "Written Law," and they trump the Oral Law. If any Oral Law violates the Written Law, it did not come from God. The Ten Commandments were not a political document inscribed in stone so that a government could be set up using the commandments as its foundation. If this were the case, God would have selected a king right there at the very spot. But no, God was giving Moses instructions to take down to the people, a list of morals to live by. Understand that these commandments or morals go back much further then the day they were delivered into the hands of Moses. Even in the book of Genesis, one will find these moral principles starting with Adam and Eve and the events that transpired after their exodus from Eden. God understood what was best for mankind, since mankind lived in an imperfect world. God understood that the individual was a scarce resource, who should value life to the fullest. Thus, through instructing mankind to care and use all that was created for them, morals and principles had to be established in order to avoid conflict.

Therefore, we shall revisit each commandment and weigh them out to understand their moral position in our quest to understand God's position on government and the role of humanity.

The First Commandment

"I am the Lord your God, who brought you out of the land of Egypt, out of the house of bondage. You shall have no other gods before Me."[5]

The first commandment is the establishment of God's ideal system, which indicates that God is the Father and Mother of humanity, the creator of a system that promotes liberty. Unlike Egypt, where one would serve the pharaoh, for the pharaoh was the state, all property was his by the will of the gods. This is because pharaoh saw himself as a god on earth.

This commandment also protects property and prohibiting the worship of other gods, which is the equivalent to a statist system. These systems do not recognize the individual's right to liberty and property. This did not mean the people could not worship other gods, but rather that God is making the statement that you cannot mix two opposing systems, expecting the same

---

[5] Exodus 20:1-3.

moral philosophy that advocates liberty and self-ownership. Such an example would be like living by the commandments of God but worshiping pharaoh as if he was a god. This would be contradicting and counterproductive, for a physical god who controls the masses owns the worker and all their production.

Therefore, the first commandment is a commandment that advocates liberty for all who abide by God's moral law. Liberty promotes peace, peace promotes productivity, and productivity creates wealth. Unlike the systems that surrounded the Hebrew people that advocated altruism through the worship of a state-personage, such as pharaoh. The first commandment that God uttered to Moses and inscribed on stone essentially establishes his form of non-government, in which God is the ultimate atheist, and therefore the first anarchist.[6]

The Second Commandment

"You shall not make for yourself a carved image, or any likeness of anything that is in heaven above, or that is in the earth beneath, or that is in the water under the earth; you shall not bow down to them nor serve them. For I, the Lord your God, am a jealous God, visiting the iniquity of the fathers on the children to the third and fourth generations of those who hate Me, but

---

[6] Exodus 20:4-6.

showing mercy to thousands, to those who love Me and keep My Commandments."[7]

The second commandment is a continuation of the first, but goes into further detail concerning images. Carved images were utilized by some cultures as a means to worship a god or goddess. In the ancient times, the Egyptians, Assyrians, and Babylonians to name a few, worshipped at the foot of these statues. In the present, the documents established by governments are no different when it comes to idol worship. Therefore, we shall discuss the two.

What makes the worship of statues bad is that the statues of these various deities represent systems of oppression. Take the god Molek, mentioned in (Leviticus 18:21); the verse states, "Do not give any of your children to be sacrificed to Molek, for you must not profane the name of your God. I am the LORD." Molek was an ancient Semitic deity worshipped by the Canaanites, Phoenicians, and even by the Hebrews at times. Those who believed in Molek believed in child sacrifice to please Molek. Some historians argue that this was voluntary, while others argue the opposite; whatever the case may be, it was still an act of murder. The person or guardian is making the choice for someone else who cannot make a conscious choice on his/her own, or that person is conscious and still has no voice in the matter. These types of altruistic systems that require the sacrifice of people to please a god are in

---

[7] Ibid.

fact taking the rights of the individual away. Self-ownership and property means nothing when the gods or goddess they worshiped require the death of a person or persons.

The majority of Christians and Jews will agree with this argument, but will point out and say Catholics bow down and worship statues. Yes, Catholics do have many statues in their churches, but it is false to assume that they bow down and worship the statues as was done in the days of old. The difference between a statue in Catholicism and a statue in ancient Babylonia is that one is worshipped while the other is not. When one takes a moment and reads John 5:39, one will see that the idea of images, whether in a temple or not, were not always worshipped. An example is found in the book of Exodus 25:18-20, in which God states:

> And thou shalt make two cherubims of gold, of beaten work shalt thou make them, in the two ends of the mercy seat. And make one cherub on the one end, and the other cherub on the other end: even of the mercy seat shall ye make the cherubims on the two ends thereof. And the cherubims shall stretch forth their wings on high, covering the mercy seat with their wings, and their faces shall look one to another;

toward the mercy seat shall the faces of the cherubims be.[8]

In addition, consider 1 Chronicles 28:18-19,[9] which deals with the temple in which David wishes to build and even gives a description of carved images such as angels. If you want something more prophetic, then look no further than to the book of Ezekiel 41:17–18,[10] which mentions that the future temple of God has carved images within the temple. Nevertheless, there are those who will use Exodus 32:31 to tell you why you are not suppose to have carved images, but what they fail to understand is that the images mentioned in Exodus 32:31 are worshipped as if they were gods.[11]

Therefore, to have carved images which are not for worship is no different from seeing family photos, or even a painted family portrait, hanging from the wall. These images are a story in view, a source of remembrance for those who are alive.

When it comes to the state, both past and present, whether the state is based on the rule of a single individual or by a body of men, those images are still a form of idol worship.

Egypt worshipped many deities including the pharaoh. Pharaoh, in the eyes of his people, was a living breathing representation of god on earth. In essence,

---

[8] Exodus 25:18-20.
[9] 1 Chronicles 28:18-19.
[10] Ezekiel 41:17–18.
[11] Exodus 32:31.

pharaoh owned everything, for he was the state, and everyone and everything owned was effectively his. Therefore, everyone under pharaoh's rule is sacrificed to his desires on the whims of his needs.

War is another example of the sacrifice to the state, in which a god, like Ares, is used to promote this practice of honor deaths by means of combat. The state will use such a practice to justify its means, for war is an extension of politics and the politics of the various societies in the ancient world and modern center on gods made of flesh, paper, and stone.

Even today, here in America, many look to the flag and give thanks and alms to this piece of material. The flag is a silent god who cannot speak, but is spoken for by a body of elected representatives as if they were the voice of God himself. Even a document like The Constitution is but a false idol, a cover that determines what is best for everyone morally when, in fact, it slowly oppresses everyone. Any government established on a document that guarantees moral rights, signed into law by a body of men, cannot guarantee rights, for when it does it automatically violates the moral prerogative of self-rule.

In summary, religion was the politics of the past, whereas politics is the religion of the present. There is no difference, except for the exchanging of gods.

The Third Commandment

"You shall not take the name of the Lord your God in vain, for the Lord will not hold him guiltless who takes His name in vain."[12]

The third commandment seems simple enough. Do not use the Lord's name in vain. Some will say the Lord's name is sacred, as in not to speak outwardly of his "true name," which some say is Yahweh, or that one should not write the name God, and if his name must be written, it should be written like G-d and not God. I find both of these in error for they are totally missing the point of the third commandment. Does anyone really know the true name of God? I think not, there are many names for God found in the Bible and besides that, he is not human and his language is unknown. But this commandment is not about how God's name will sound or how one shall spell it. The third commandment is when one uses his name recklessly, as in determining what God thinks without knowing what he wills or what his principles are.

An example would be the notion that God loves the idea of the state, or that God loves my religion more than yours. Both are wrong, but billions of people do not understand that God favors neither. Additionally, the third commandment informs us on the issue of property. God is

---

[12] Exodus 20:7.

also saying that he protects property both private and personal. By prohibiting us from using his name to justify ideas, which may sound "righteous," by saying it is the "will of God" that we attack another country or that we have the moral obligation to kill those people, for they do not believe as we do and were found ungodly. The fact of the matter is that our will is not God's will, especially if it is contrary to his morals and principles which he created for us to live by.

Therefore, the third commandment is not about taking his name in vain, but rather abusing his name in vain by speaking for him as if he wills what you will, especially if the intent is to harm and take what is not yours under the guise that "God wills it!"

The Fourth Commandment

"Remember the Sabbath day, to keep it holy. Six days you shall labor and do all your work, but the seventh day is the Sabbath of the Lord your God. In it you shall do no work: you, nor your son, nor your daughter, nor your male servant, nor your female servant, nor your cattle, nor your stranger who is within your gates. For in six days the Lord made the heavens and the earth, the sea, and all that is in them, and rested the seventh day. Therefore the Lord blessed the Sabbath day and hallowed it.[13]

---

[13] Exodus 20:10.

The fourth commandment is by far the most controversial of the Ten Commandments when it comes to a day of worship. If one does a search on the subject, one will notice the countless articles and books concerning the Sunday Sabbath debate, particularly among Christians. One side said it has changed to Sunday because of Christ's resurrection from the dead, while the other side says he did not rise on a Sunday and, therefore, the Sabbath is still the day in which one should worship. Others will say if he did rise on a Sunday, it still would not matter, for there is no commandment found in the Bible that changes the day from Sabbath to Sunday.

Now, I am not going to get into the issues concerning which day is correct, but rather what the day meant. Therefore, I will fall back on Romans 14:5-6, and agree that people should let people be. In other words, "live and let live" for there is no point in squabbling over the day of worship, but rather focus on its intention.

Many will look at the fourth commandment and agree that it means rest from work as mentioned. Rest is important in order to recover from the day-to-day activities done throughout the workweek, whether physical or mental. Therefore, God is acknowledging that the body is a scarce resource of value and needs rest. If you own land, what good is your land or the resources you provide if your body is not well in order to provide the essential items needed daily? Regardless of landownership, the body still needs rest since productivity does not necessarily mean one has to own land as a means to acquire wealth.

When God spoke these words to Moses, remember that the Hebrew people were a semi-nomadic agricultural society during this period. It was not until they had finally reached the "Promised Land" that they became full time property owners.

In today's world, we still have people whose livelihoods are based on agricultural production. The same goes for those who work not in the business of farming, but rather from home or in the city, working in some factory or office sector.

Therefore, the issue is simple; jobs, duties, and ideas change ever so constantly. But one thing is for certain, the human body needs rest, for it is a scarce resource that has the ability to provide a service that creates wealth. The Sabbath was made for mankind to take a break in order to keep progress flowing at a healthy rate.

The Fifth Commandment

"Honor your father and your mother, that your days may be long upon the land which the Lord your God is giving you."[14]

To honor your parents is a moral obligation just as it is a moral obligation for your parents to honor you. It works both ways.

---

[14] Exodus 20:12.

The fifth commandment is obvious and its meaning is quite clear. However, it also has another message, and that is property rights. This commandment not only protects the property owned by the parents or elderly, but also ensures that very property will pass down to their children. Whether it is land or personal items that are passed down is of no matter, for property is property and the rightful heir to the property is the offspring the parents produced or even adopted.

This commandment warns that if you steal from your parents, you need to understand that the sins of the father may pass on to the children. In other words, your children will observe your actions and may very well repeat them. Thus, to ensure ownership, God made it very clear that if you are to own property, be sure to respect the property of your parents, for one day you will inherit it. You should also respect the property of others not related to you in order to keep the peace within the community.

This commandment ensures that the property, whether owned or not, should be respected, for property, no matter its use or function, is still property to someone and it holds value to those who hold it dear.

The Sixth Commandment

"You shall not murder."[15]

---

[15] Exodus 20:13.

The sixth commandment is obvious. If you murder, you have unlawfully justified a death. A person who is willing to take a life or many lives through the act of murder shows a lack of respect for life.

Therefore, that person should expect no respect. To murder is to destroy a scarce resource. The person murdered most likely provided a valuable resource to the family and community, physically, mentally, and emotionally, for the individual is a combination of self-ownership, as well as an owner of physical property.

God understood that if we respect one another, we will get along better, and if we get along, we can live our lives in peace without considering destruction to ourselves or to others, for murder disrupts production and inheritance and takes what is precious to us and that is life.

The Seventh Commandment

"You shall not commit adultery."[16]

Marriage is a mutual contract. To break that contract with another violates the boundaries that were established.

I am not going to get into all the various issues dealing with marriage in the Bible, such as multiple wives or whether they were considered property, or other issues, but rather discuss the moral and financial obligation

---

[16] Exodus 20:14.

agreed to when it comes to marriage and what happens when one commits adultery.

There are many reasons why people cheat on their spouse. Such reasons given are a lack of connection, lack of emotional or maybe financial support, boredom, and the list goes on. None of the reasons mentioned is right. It would be better off to first nullify the marriage before proceeding any further. To cheat on your spouse is breaking a contract.

Another reason why breaking the marriage contract is bad is due to property issues. Both hold a title to property. When one commits adultery, one is allowing another to trespass. Property of the heart and material property items are at stake. Losing one's heart is just as bad, if not worse, than losing one's physical items.

Therefore, adultery in our time, as it was in their time, was about the breaching of faith between the husband and wife.

The Eighth Commandment

"You shall not steal."[17]

The eighth commandment protects physical property across the board. Taking anything that another person physically owns which is not yours is stealing. To take property away from another is taking a valuable

---

[17] Exodus 20:15.

resource from the victim, even if the object is not beneficial to the creation of wealth. This commandment ensures the protection of all forms of physical property.

The Ninth Commandment

"You shall not bear false witness against your neighbor."[18]

Providing a false testimony not only hurts the person or persons you are confronting, it could lead to the destruction of a person's reputation, thus causing alienation among the community and possibly with the family, which leads to possible strife that was not needed. Moreover, this commandment also protects property and possession from accusations that are deemed not true, ensuring the property of the person, or persons, remains in their possession.

The Tenth Commandment

"You shall not covet your neighbor's house; you shall not covet your neighbor's wife, nor his male servant, nor his female servant, nor his ox, nor his donkey, nor anything that is your neighbor's."[19]

---

[18] Exodus 20:16.
[19] Exodus 20:17.

The tenth commandment sums up the other nine commandments in which it protects property on all levels, whether it is a person's body or the objects he owns.

There is a misconception concerning the tenth commandment by many Christians and people of no faith. That misconception is that coveting means to want what others have. This is not true. Seeing something you would like to own, such as a certain food, clothes, or car, does not mean that you covet it. Actually, this is far from coveting; to see something you like in a store window or on TV is nothing more than admiring the object, and there is nothing wrong with buying the object, if you can afford it.

What the tenth commandment is getting at is that it is wrong to covet, not to admire and want. To covet is a negative desire, another form of lust that may lead to theft and that is deemed unacceptable. The thievery requires methods which will harm another in some form, whether physically or financially, if the action is taken.

The Ten Commandments in the New Testament

There are those who say Jesus and the apostles were socialist or proto-communist; thus, Jesus and the apostles were for social justice. None of these is true. If Jesus supported such an ideology, in which the state had an obligation to its citizens, as in taking care and ensuring everything was redistributed equally, then why did Jesus support and uphold the Ten Commandments?

25

Now, I'm not going to go through all the Ten Commandments, but rather the commandments which Jesus mentions that conflict with the state.

The Ten Commandments are proof that God hates the state and is pro liberty. Why else would he have written the Ten Commandments in stone? These ten laws are the very foundation that protects the individual and his property. Therefore, if God hates the state, does Jesus hate the state?

In the book of Matthew 22:37-38 Jesus says, "Thou shalt love the Lord thy God with all thy heart, and with all thy soul, and with thy entire mind. This is the first and great commandment."[20] Jesus is clearly mentioning the first commandment that, "You shall have no other gods before Me."[21] If you love God, you love liberty. To chase after other gods would be worshipping the state, for all other gods are state sponsored whether religious or secular.

Jesus also mentions the second commandment, in which he states, "God is Spirit, and those who worship Him must worship in spirit and truth."[22] As the saying goes, "the truth shall make you free."[23] Truth has no image, but governments along with religious institutions, will provide a false image, an aid, or an object, which deceives people into thinking that God must support this country, or that country, or any country for that matter, for

---

[20] Matthew 22:37-38. See also Luke 4:8 & Matthew 4:10.
[21] Exodus 20:3
[22] John 4:24.
[23] John 8:32.

they say they speak the truth. When in fact, God is no respecter of persons, for all are equal under the moral law and governmental titles mean nothing as Jesus indicated. A government holds a monopoly over life, liberty, property, and prosperity. Therefore, statism creates the crime, just as it was in the time of Jesus as it is today.

Jesus also spoke against murder, for to murder someone is to take life; thus murdering is an act of stealing, "You shall not steal."[24] This is not only applied to a person murdering another person, but is primarily applied to the state, which is notorious for looting the public's pockets and destroying private property at home or abroad, resulting in the deaths of millions!

As already mentioned, if you murder, you are guilty of breaking the eight commandment that Jesus mentions often in the books of Matthew 5:21-22, 15:19-20, 19:18, and in Mark 7:21, 23 and 10:19. In Matthew 15:3, Jesus states, "Why do you also transgress the commandment of God because of your tradition?" Jesus goes on to use a quote from the Prophet Isaiah "This people honors Me with their lips, But their heart is far from Me, And in vain they worship Me, Teaching as doctrines the commandments of men. For laying aside the commandment of God, you hold the tradition of men." Jesus's statement is blunt and to the point.

The majority of people in Jesus's time are no different than today. They support a state system that in no way reflects the principles or commandments of God.

---

[24] Exodus 20:15.

Instead, they use his name like many politicians and preachers do today. They will stand before humanity and promote policies they think God or Jesus would approve, such as war, taxes, unjust laws, social welfare systems...etc. In every way, they preach liberty with their lips but do not dare allow liberty to thrive. Not only do they break the sixth commandment and eighth commandment in a political and governmental way, they break all the commandments of God!

Jesus's message is simple, if you want to break free then give up and opt out of the state, let go of the state, break free from the chains of injustice, and live!

The Ten Commandments in Summary

In essence, the Ten Commandments promote the idea of a stateless society based on moral laws that protect the property of the person, including the person's body.

The idea was fresh in many ways. When the Israelites came out of Egypt, they had just left a tyrannical system in which all belonged to the pharaoh. Thus, after many generations, the Israelites would accept many aspects of the state as we do today; it becomes ingrained in our lives, and it becomes harder to break free from the idea that we need rulers to provide the essentials of life.

Therefore, to come out of that type of system and go into one that promotes liberty would have been a struggle, just as it is today. When you ask a person if they would prefer a stateless, private law society, you will receive mixed answers with mixed looks. When explained to them what that means, many people think that a government is still necessary and that we need a leader along with a body of representatives to decide what is best for us without ever asking us.

Many people seem to have awakened from their slumber of acceptance and now are beginning to question the role of government—just like the Israelites. However, it was a different situation for the Israelites; they crash-landed into it. They had a choice: it was either live free or die. The Israelites chose to live and were on the run as they defended their liberty. We, on the other hand, have had the luxury of being free, but our liberties have slowly been eradicated—if not extinguished entirely. Most of today's population has had to take baby steps back into the very idea of what liberty means. But even those who have put a foot forward still embrace statism. It is hard to imagine what the Israelites were thinking when they heard the first commandment, which trumps the state and all the baggage that comes with it. But then again, it is easy to imagine, just ask a stranger if he or she would like to abolish government.

The first commandment on the surface suggests that God is king, but when the commandments are viewed together, they indicate that it is not so much about God being king, but rather the principles and morals advocated by God due to our physical makeup.

Therefore, the Ten Commandments tell us that God is just a guide, a teacher, a parent, but it takes people to listen and to understand what God is promoting. Thus, the commandments that were passed down to the Israelites at Mount Sinai guaranteed that each individual is a king, since the commandments promote liberty through the act of individualism.

Some Christians and Jews may find this odd or blasphemies, but we must ask ourselves what matters most to God? Any person can worship God, but most people do not understand what God values most. Therefore, if we are to acknowledge what God values utmost, we not only honor him, we also honor our neighbor. This is most important because the two greatest commandments spoken by Jesus sums up the Ten Commandments of God. In Matthew 22:37-40, Jesus states:

> Jesus said unto him, Thou shalt love the Lord thy God with all thy heart, and with all thy soul, and with all thy mind. This is the first and great commandment. And the second is like unto it, Thou shalt love thy neighbour as thyself. On these two commandments hang all the law and the prophets.[25]

After reading over the Ten Commandments, reviewing each principle the commandments offer and weighing them together, the next question to ask is, does God hate the state?

---

[25] Matthew 22:37-40. See also Deuteronomy 6:5 and Leviticus 19:18.

Chapter 4

Does God Hate the State?

The worship of the state is the worship of force. There is no more dangerous menace to civilization than a government of incompetent, corrupt, or vile men. The worst evils which mankind ever had to endure were inflicted by bad governments. —Ludwig von Mises[26]

During the time of Adam and Eve, there was no king or queen, but then again, both Adam and Eve were in charge of the earth for they were the only two. Once they had children and their children had children, we still see individualism reign supreme. However, we know little of the events that transpired after a certain amount of generations had come into being and before the great flood. On the other hand, we do read of a certain person establishing a city as mentioned in Genesis 4:17 "And Cain knew his wife; and she conceived, and bore Enoch: and he built a city, and called the name of the city after the name of his son, Enoch." Establishing a city does not necessarily mean a form of government was established along with it, but given the fact that it was Cain who established a city, it is quite possible that the world's first murderer may have

---

[26] Ludwig von Mises, *Omnipotent Government* (Auburn, AL: Ludwig von Mises Institute, 1985), 49.

also been the world's first statist. Unfortunately, we know nothing concerning what types or type of pre-government that was in place before the great flood.

During the time of Abraham, there was still no king, but those with him lived freely without a government. When the Israelites left Egypt, they still had no king. During the time of Judges, the Israelites still had no king, but one day changed all that, and you will be reading about shortly.

Therefore, it should be considered that God was not their king, but rather his principles allowed mankind to reign as royalty, so long as they treated each other equally and understood his moral law of liberty, which was not always the case. But God understood that the process of freeing oneself from regimes and systems that were unnatural to the free spirit of man would be a gradual understanding as man moved forward through history. God was not going to drag them to freedom, but rather God used choice and consequences to open their eyes to the possibility of freedom by allowing choice and consequences to be their guide.

The Tower of Babel

"Now the whole earth had one language and one speech."
—Genesis 11:1

The story of the Tower of Babel, which most of us heard in a church sermon or discussed among ourselves, is usually misunderstood. One conversation I had in the past concerning why the tower was built revealed that mankind was trying to reach and invade Heaven to commit an act of deicide. Another explanation was that the people building the tower wanted to reach the Heavens to be like God, to show they are equal to God, demonstrating that he was not needed for they are God. A symbolic act nonetheless. Nevertheless, the Bible does not say that was the motive.

In the book of Genesis 11:1 it states, "Now the whole earth had one language and one speech." When Noah and his family opened the door to come outside the Ark, they all spoke one language. Once they established homes and broke soil to plant crops, the people began to multiply over time. It was not too long after that the people decided they wanted a centralized government. The man to lead these people was none other than Nimrod. The only issue with this is that the Bible does not say it was Nimrod who overlooked the construction of the Tower of Babel. Yet we find in Genesis 10:8-12, starting in verse 10, "And the beginning of his kingdom was Babel, and Erech, and Accad, and Calneh, in the land of Shinar."[27] This verse establishes Nimrod as the one who overlooked the construction of the tower, but this is debatable.

According to the Bible, Nimrod was the son of Cush and great-grandson of Noah. The name of Nimrod means "rebel" and rebel they did, starting with Genesis 11:2-9, which it states:

---

[27] Genesis 10:8-12.

And it came to pass, as they journeyed from the east, that they found a plain in the land of Shinar, and they dwelt there. Then they said to one another, "Come, let us make bricks and bake them thoroughly." They had brick for stone, and they had asphalt for mortar. And they said, "Come, let us build ourselves a city, and a tower whose top is in the heavens; let us make a name for ourselves, lest we be scattered abroad over the face of the whole earth." But the LORD came down to see the city and the tower which the sons of men had built. And the LORD said, "Indeed the people are one and they all have one language, and this is what they begin to do; now nothing that they propose to do will be withheld from them. Come, let us go down and there confuse their language, that they may not understand one another's speech." So the LORD scattered them abroad from there over the face of all the earth, and they ceased building the city. Therefore its name is called Babel, because there the LORD confused the language of all the earth; and from there the LORD scattered them abroad over the face of all the earth.[28]

---

[28] Genesis 11:2-9.

The people led by Nimrod are organized, they speak one language, and they are looking to establish a centralized government in which Nimrod can control mankind through oppressive authority. In order to do this, Nimrod needs to build a city, a power base in which all trade, taxes, and needs flow into the city; Nimrod's goal is to hold a monopoly, not only over the goods and services, but over mankind as well. Man is no more than an object to control and to beat. Therefore, Nimrod looks to establish a foundation of destruction. Unfortunately, this foundation is still alive today in the form of political ideology. However, for this one brief moment, God stops mankind from centralizing, by confusing the languages so they cannot collectively build and supply one man the needs to do whatever he wants. This confusion of languages only temporarily halts the process towards a unified central power, but it also weakens this power by centralizing it to the respected languages now created.

God's Last Judge

"In those days Israel had no king; everyone did as he saw fit."
—Judges 21:25

In the book of 1 Samuel 8:10-18 God warned the Israelites through the prophet Samuel and said:

So Samuel told all the words of the Lord to the people who asked him for a king. And he said, "This will be the behavior of the king who will reign over you: He will take your sons and appoint them for his own chariots and to be his horsemen, and some will run before his chariots. He will appoint captains over his thousands and captains over his fifties, will set some to plow his ground and reap his harvest, and some to make his weapons of war and equipment for his chariots. He will take your daughters to be perfumers, cooks, and bakers. And he will take the best of your fields, your vineyards, and your olive groves, and give them to his servants. He will take a tenth of your grain and your vintage, and give it to his officers and servants. And he will take your male servants, your female servants, your finest young men, and your donkeys, and put them to his work. He will take a tenth of your sheep. And you will be his servants. And you will cry out in that day because of your king whom you have chosen for yourselves, and the Lord will not hear you in that day.[29]

---

[29] 1 Samuel 8:10-18.

The question we have to ask is why did the Israelites want a king? Our answer lies in the book of 1 Samuel 8:1-3, which states:

> Now it came to pass when Samuel was old that he made his sons judges over Israel. The name of his firstborn was Joel, and the name of his second, Abijah; they were judges in Beersheba. But his sons did not walk in his ways; they turned aside after dishonest gain, took bribes, and perverted justice.[30]

Notice that Samuel is appointing his sons to be judges over Israel. The problem with this is that God was the one who appoints the judge for Israel from time-to-time, but no man is allowed to appoint his son to be next in line as a judge of Israel unless God says so.[31] Nevertheless, Samuel takes it upon himself and appoints his sons; his sons turn out to be dishonest by taking advantage of the people.

Because of the dishonest actions by his sons, the elders of Israel gathered at Ramah, spoke to Samuel, and said, "Look, you are old, and your sons do not walk in your ways. Now make us a king to judge us like all the nations."[32]

---

[30] 1 Samuel 8:1-3.

[31] Thomas Nelson, *The NKJV Study Bible: Second Edition* (Nashville, TN: Thomas Nelson, Inc, 2007), 430.

[32] 1 Samuel 8:4-5.

The Israelites want a king to rule over them, but seem not to understand that a king will rob them just as Samuel's sons did yet the robbery will be much worse.

> But the thing displeased Samuel when they said, "Give us a king to judge us." So Samuel prayed to the Lord. And the Lord said to Samuel, "Heed the voice of the people in all that they say to you; for they have not rejected you, but they have rejected Me, that I should not reign over them. According to all the works which they have done since the day that I brought them up out of Egypt, even to this day; with which they have forsaken Me and served other gods; so they are doing to you also."[33]

Samuel's anger and disappointment is understood, your sons have led sinful lives and now the people want a system that is the opposite of liberty. This tells us that the Israelites have forgotten their struggle in history to overcome those who wish to submit them under oppressive rule. It may also tell us that the elders themselves have become corrupt and are seeking power for themselves. God then goes on to tell Samuel, "Now therefore, heed their voice. However, you shall solemnly forewarn them, and show them the behavior of the king

---

[33] 1 Samuel 8:6-8.

who will reign over them."[34] The elders will hear none of it and demand that liberty be replaced with the seed that will eventually grow into tyranny. This request by the elders to God leads us back to 1 Samuel 8:10-18 as mentioned earlier.

In summary, it is obvious from the surface of the scriptures. The elders were tired of the corruption of Samuels's sons whom Samuel appointed as judges over Israel, by in which he had no authority to do so. However, those affected by Samuel's sons took their gripe forward to the elders of Israel, which in turn the elders confronted Samuel and rejected God. God warned the elders what would happen if they established a king, but the elders would hear none of it and the people whom they represented may have just wanted justice, whereas the elders saw this as an opportunity to grab power. Nevertheless, the elders refused to reason in thinking through their request and said:

> No, but we will have a king over us, that we also may be like all the nations, and that our king may judge us and go out before us and fight our battles." And Samuel heard all the words of the people, and he repeated them in the hearing of the Lord. So the Lord said to Samuel, "Heed their voice, and make

---

[34] 1 Samuel 8:9.

them a king." And Samuel said to the men
of Israel, "Every man go to his city."[35]

What the elders discussed within their respected tribes is
unknown. No one knows how the elders spun it to the
people. Nevertheless, what can be said with certainty is
that they did not understand how much of their liberties
they were about to lose on all fronts once a king was
established. But it is interesting to note that the elders
wanted to be like other nations, whereas God wanted them
to be a nation of priests.[36] In other words, God's hope was
that the Israelites become a nation of priests, who would
preach and live by the law of liberty, and be a peaceful
light unto all people. So now, back to the question, does
God hate the state? The answer is yes, God hates the
system. God hates how the system forces its will upon the
people for the state only takes and never creates; it
presents a false liberty through collectivism by replacing
liberty with gradual slavery. God knew what would
happen once a government would be established and,
unfortunately, it seems that Israel forgot its history as
indicated in the book of 1 Samuel 8:19-22. Mankind does
forget at times no matter how euphoric the feeling is at
first, those who are born next may lose a little
understanding, but as time moves forward, each
generation forgets even more, until another generation
gets it, thereby challenging the previous generation.

---

[35] 1 Samuel 8:19-22.
[36] Exodus 19:6.

Chapter 5

Does God favor Tithing and Taxes?

In today's modern world, as it was before, governments have always collected taxes for the greater good of society, or so their leaders say. The same can be applied to religious organizations, as well. Many churches, like many governments, ask or demand for money in order to function. If you pay taxes to the government, you will avoid jail, thus safeguarding your family from any suffering the government would cause had you not paid. In some religious establishments, the more you paid, the greater the blessing. Thus, you safeguard the well-being of your family spiritually. Both are false and do nothing for your well-being other then robbing you of your hard earnings.

I understand that in a church giving is voluntary, at least at most of them, but the pressure is on as they pass the basket around among the congregation. Nevertheless, most people do not give it a second thought if you do not place money in the basket, but some people do watch and notice what is put into the basket. Now, I do not know what people are thinking, nor am I implying that they are taking mental notes, but some do talk among themselves as to who could have afforded to put more in or who is just showing off. Personally, I have heard these comments, so don't say it doesn't happen. Nevertheless, according to ministers, the more you give, the bigger the blessing you shall receive as previously mentioned. Not all ministers say this but some do, and many people in church also believe that what you give, you shall get back in blessings from God. Is this correct is this right?

The answer is no! Tithing or taxes, whichever you prefer to call it, are one-tenth part of something. But what most people forget is that it is totally voluntary.

Tithing in the Old Testament

In the book of Genesis, we find no obligation to give something of value unless you voluntarily do so, as in the case of Abraham, but Abraham's gift was a onetime offer. In the book of Genesis chapter 14, we read that Abraham's nephew, Lot, was taken captive along with his property by Elamite forces that defeated the king of Sodom. After the Elamites took the property of Lot, they settled him and his family outside the Kingdom of Sodom. When Abraham received word that Lot and his household had been taken captive, Abraham quickly assembled a fighting force of 318 men. Abraham and his volunteers set out on a night raid and were successful in their endeavor. They killed the king of Elam, rescued Lot, along with his household and property, and brought back the spoils of war. Afterwards, Abraham would give a tenth of the spoils to Melchizedek, king of Salem (Jerusalem), for both honored the same God and Abraham was his guest.

Abraham was returning the gift due to Melchizedek's hospitality, while the king of Sodom made an offer to let Abraham keep all the possessions captured from the Elamites for his great deed. Abraham declined to keep the possessions. Instead, he returned the captives and spoils to the king of Sodom. Abraham accomplished what he set out to do and that was to rescue his nephew Lot, along with his household.[37]

Another example of voluntary giving would be Abraham's grandson, Jacob.

> Then Jacob made a vow, saying, "If God will be with me and will watch over me on this journey I am taking and will give me food to eat and clothes to wear so that I return safely to my father's household, then the LORD will be my God and this stone that I have set up as a pillar will be God's house, and of all that you give me I will give you a tenth."[38]

Notice the word "If" in the passage. Jacob was making a voluntary contract between him and God "If God will be with me," I will do as he says and, in return for his blessings, I will give an offering back. This tithe is voluntary and is between Jacob and God alone. In addition, Jacob is not forcing those who accompany him

---

[37] Genesis 14:1-24.
[38] Genesis 28:20–22.

into giving either. If those among Jacob wish to make a contract with God, they are free to do so but are under no obligation, nor does God request a tithe.

In the book of Exodus, we find tithing to be voluntary once again, but not for long. When the Israelites finally left Egypt after taking their share of the spoils of war, due to being "corvée labor,"[39] God requested nothing from them. There is no mentioning of the Israelites giving a tenth of their spoils as a tithe after the events had passed in Egypt. Even at Mount Sinai, where they received the Ten Commandments, there still was no request by God for any tithe. When one reads Exodus 20:19 & 24:18,[40] understand that these four chapters are recorded in the Book of the Covenant, notice that the covenant had been established between God and the Israelites, all that was written is final and no other laws came directly from God, nor is there a mentioning of a tithe requested in the Book of the Covenant.

The first request is made is a voluntary request by Moses.

> They came, both men and women, as many
> as had a willing heart, and brought earrings
> and nose rings, rings and necklaces, all

---

[39] Richard A. Gabriel, *The Military History of Ancient Israel* (Westport, Conn: Praeger, 2003), 62.
[40] Exodus 20:19 & 24:18.

jewelry of gold, that is, every man who made an offering of gold to the LORD.[41]

The children of Israel brought a freewill offering to the LORD, all the men and women whose hearts were willing to bring material for all kinds of work which the LORD, by the hand of Moses, had commanded to be done.[42]

And they received from Moses all the offering which the children of Israel had brought for the work of the service of making the sanctuary. So they continued bringing to him freewill offerings every morning.[43]

For the material they had was sufficient for all the work to be done—indeed too much.[44]

As you can read, Moses instructed the need for building a Tabernacle and items were requested for this purpose. But notice that no person was forced into give such items. For words like, "willing heart" and "freewill" indicated that a tithe was not an obligation but rather a voluntary one, no harm, no foul.

---

[41] Exodus 35:22.

[42] Exodus 35:29.

[43] Exodus 36:3.

[44] Exodus 36:7.

After Sinai and into the Promised Land

There are those who will say one is obligated to pay tithes to the church. They will use Biblical passages, such as Leviticus 27:30; Numbers 18:26; Deuteronomy 14:24, and 2 Chronicles 31:5. The problem with this is that the Israelites would pay 10% or their tithes, but one often forgets that the Israelites paid "multiple tithes," in which the amount being paid far exceeds 10% and is more like 23% and some change. Most forget that the Israelites paid a Levitical tithe, Numbers 18:20-21, a Festival tithe, Deuteronomy 12:1-19 and 14:22-26, and finally a Poor tithe, Deuteronomy 14:28-29 and 26:12-13.

Another issue that churches often forget is that the tithe was paid, not by money, but rather with food.[45] The Israelites were an agrarian based society and their wealth derived from the food they produced. If churches still believe that the tithe has been changed from offering food to now offering money, what authority does the minister have to collect tithes when he is not a Levite? Even if he was a Levite, what authority does he have when Christ abolished the Old Testament system?

The Levites collected tithes because they did not own land like the other tribes. "The priests, the Levites— all the tribe of Levi—shall have no part nor inheritance with Israel; they shall eat the offerings of the LORD made

---

[45]Deuteronomy 14:22-23. See also Deuteronomy 18:1-5, Deuteronomy 26:12.

by fire, and His portion."[46] The Levites did own property, of course, in the villages and towns "For the children of Joseph were two tribes: Manasseh and Ephraim. And they gave no part to the Levites in the land, except cities to dwell in, with their common-lands for their livestock and their property."[47]

The Mosaic Law did establish a temporary tithing system, but one has to be careful for these tithes were not law, as in the sense that one must tithe or else. If tithing was mandatory in the Old Testament after Sinai, then explain the poor and needy. The poor and needy have nothing to offer to the Levites or to anyone else for that matter, and if the poor and needy could not pay, then those with wealth could back out in giving in one or all the tithes mentioned earlier. Here is why. Earlier in the book, I discussed 1 Samuel 8:10-18 in which the Israelites wanted a king and a state like their neighbors. God warned what would be tithed starting in 1 Samuel 8:14-15 and 17. "And he will take the best of your fields, your vineyards, and your olive groves, and give them to his servants. He will take a tenth of your grain and your vintage, and give it to his officers and servants. He will take a tenth of your sheep." From these three verses, tithing may have become mandatory once the state of Israel was established, along with a king and a standing army. To make a further argument that tithing was not mandatory but purely voluntary, in the days before kings and after Sinai, notice

---

[46] Deuteronomy 18:1.
[47] Joshua 14:4.

the last verse in the book of Judges 21:25. "In those days there was no king in Israel; everyone did what was right in his own eyes."[48] Therefore, if this verse is true as in depicting an accurate description of the Israelites, then both tithing and the observance of the oral law were voluntary.

Jesus and Taxes

Of the many ministers I have heard and spoken with in my years, every one of them said that Jesus paid his taxes at some point during the year. I decided to ask a few ministers a long time ago about Jesus and the tax issue. When I asked if Jesus was against taxation, I would get a big fat NO! Of course, the ministers must say no, because to say yes would mean they would lose tithes to their church, which is a form of income through taxation. A few ministers would point to me and tell me to read Matthew 17:24-27.

> When they had come to Capernaum, those who received the temple tax came to Peter and said, "Does your Teacher not pay the temple tax?" He said, "Yes."And when he had come into the house, Jesus anticipated him, saying, "What do you think, Simon? From whom do the kings of the earth take

---

[48] Judges 21:25

customs or taxes, from their sons or from strangers?" Peter said to Him, "From strangers." Jesus said to him, "Then the sons are free. Nevertheless, lest we offend them, go to the sea, cast in a hook, and take the fish that comes up first. And when you have opened its mouth, you will find a piece of money; take that and give it to them for Me and you."[49]

This was the first passages shown to me. But what the minister and the various ministers who preach this in support of taxation forget is that Jesus had to pay a temple tax. Jesus had to pay the temple tax for he was not looking for trouble, not because he felt it was the right thing to do, but because he had to fulfill the prophecy spoken about him in the Old Testament.

Matthew 22:15-22 is probably my favorite passage concerning taxes and the one that is most clear. Many ministers use this as a reason to explain why we must pay taxes to the government.

Then the Pharisees went and plotted how they might entangle Him in His talk. And they sent to Him their disciples with the Herodians, saying, "Teacher, we know that You are true, and teach the way of God in truth; nor do You care about anyone, for

---

[49] Matthew 17:24-27.

You do not regard the person of men. Tell us, therefore, what do You think? Is it lawful to pay taxes to Caesar, or not?" But Jesus perceived their wickedness, and said, "Why do you test Me, you hypocrites? Show Me the tax money." So they brought Him a denarius. And He said to them, "Whose image and inscription is this?" They said to Him, "Caesar's." And He said to them, "Render therefore to Caesar the things that are Caesar's, and to God the things that are God's." When they had heard these words, they marveled, and left Him and went their way.[50]

The Pharisees were trying to pull one on Jesus as in a trick to see what he would say. If Jesus were to say no, he would have been arrested for rebelling against Rome, but if Jesus were to say yes, he would look as if he approved of the Roman occupation over Judea. However, Jesus caught onto the trick and instead told them "Render therefore to Caesar the things that are Caesar's, and to God the things that are God's." This is a clear rhetorical misdirection of the question and Jesus shows his brilliance by answering the Pharisees in that manner. This was Jesus' way of saying to give Caesar back his phony property. Caesar has no authority to tax us, no more than he has the authority to tax anyone else. It is a silly image of a man who collects

---

[50] Matthew 22:15-22.

stolen property in his own name. Jesus understood quite clearly just because someone writes a name on a piece of paper or has his image stamped into a coin does not give them the authority to extort you of your possessions.

If this is not convincing, consider the Apostle Matthew, who happened to be a tax collector.

> As Jesus passed on from there, He saw a man named Matthew sitting at the tax office. And He said to him, "Follow Me." So he arose and followed Him. Now it happened, as Jesus sat at the table in the house, that behold, many tax collectors and sinners came and sat down with Him and His disciples. And when the Pharisees saw it, they said to His disciples, "Why does your Teacher eat with tax collectors and sinners?" When Jesus heard that, He said to them, "Those who are well have no need of a physician, but those who are sick. But go and learn what this means: 'I desire mercy and not sacrifice.' For I did not come to call the righteous, but sinners, to repentance."[51]

What is interesting is that the Pharisees made a distinction between the two for they refer to both; whereas, Jesus lumps them together as one. Jesus said, "For I did not come to call the righteous, but sinners, to repentance." The

---

[51] Matthew 9:9-13. See also Hosea 6:6, Mark 2:14-17; Luke 5:27-32.

Pharisees seemed at odds with the tax collectors but did not consider collecting taxes as a sin; whereas, Jesus makes it quite clear that he is against taxes. In a sense, if the Pharisees could not figure out where Jesus stood on the issue of taxes when he said, "Render therefore to Caesar the things that are Caesar's, and to God the things that are God's," then they would have to know at that moment when he compared the tax collector to the sinner. Matthew, who was a tax collector, understood the message and left his job, for it was best to live free rather than participate in a system of thievery. But, what about after Christ's death, did the Apostles preach the same message?

The Apostle Paul on Government and Taxes

After the death and resurrection of Jesus, the Apostles went on to spread the good message. When it comes to whether or not the Apostles believed that one should pay taxes, some ministers will point and say, "Let every soul be subject to the governing authorities. For there is no authority except from God, and the authorities that exist are appointed by God."[52] This passage is used to support the notion that we must pay taxes and obey the government. But what if we take this verse and apply it to what has been left out.

---

[52] Romans 13:1.

Therefore whoever resists the authority resists the ordinance of God, and those who resist will bring judgment on themselves. For rulers are not a terror to good works, but to evil. Do you want to be unafraid of the authority? Do what is good, and you will have praise from the same. For he is God's minister to you for good. But if you do evil, be afraid; for he does not bear the sword in vain; for he is God's minister, an avenger to execute wrath on him who practices evil. Therefore you must be subject, not only because of wrath but also for conscience' sake. For because of this you also pay taxes, for they are God's ministers attending continually to this very thing. Render therefore to all their due: taxes to whom taxes are due, customs to whom customs, fear to whom fear, honor to whom honor.[53]

To say these passages advocate that a person, or a society for that matter, should pay taxes and obey the government would be in error. Paul is saying the exact opposite. Paul's message is a statement of outright rebellion to the ruling authorities. Paul is saying two things. The first is that even if the government were good, they would praise the message and drop their laws in favor of God's Ten

[53] Romans 13:2-7.

Commandments, thus ensuring individual property rights. But, it would go further in that those holding the power of authority would understand to let go of that authority and to decentralize, for to have authority over a body of people can only cause mischief by the person or persons who wield the power so long as it exists.

There are those who will say that we must submit because it says, "Therefore whoever resists the authority resists the ordinance of God, and those who resist will bring judgment on themselves."[54] What is misunderstood by most is that God appoints whom he deems fit. Therefore, God does not appoint tyrants and dictators. Rarely has God appointed anyone and he never agrees with how the "appointee" runs the nation, as in the case when Israel had kings. God appointed Saul, David, and Solomon, but after that, only few got the nod from the Most High.

So, why would God appoint a person to do harm over a nation, which could spill over into the neighboring nation? He doesn't. God knows the heart of man; therefore, all of mankind is deemed unworthy to hold authority over an individual or a body of people. Yes, God did appoint Saul and so forth, but only because he kept his promise to those who grumbled to Samuel. In a sense, it was God's way of letting his children have what they wanted, since the children knew better than God, or so they thought. What God does say concerning the issue of authority is this, "They set up kings, but not by Me; They

---

[54] Romans 13:1-2.

made princes, but I did not acknowledge them."[55] What Paul makes clear and what God said through Hosea is simple, if God declares an authority, he will do so himself. But, as Biblical history has shown, God is no respecter of men, especially those who abuse power. God has hired everything from individuals, to judges, and to prophets, but he despises the notion of rulers and rightfully so.

Therefore, the authority of which Paul speaks would be placed in the hands of the individual to choose what is best for his life, and God's commandments promote that very idea. Liberty is about risk taking, whether good or bad, and no government has the moral responsibility or right to choose for you. Only you can choose what is best for you, for you are the ruler of yourself.

The second aspect of Paul's message is one based on "legal positivism." James Redford states, "Legal positivism is the doctrine that whichever gang is best able to overpower others with arms and might and thereby subjugate the populace and who then proceed to proclaim themselves the 'authority' are on that account the rightful 'Authority.'"[56] Paul understood that he had to write the letter in such a way that confused or misinterpreted the Christian view on authority as to not expose themselves fully to the Roman authorities; the Christians at the time would have understood Paul's message clearly.

---

[55] Hosea 8:4.

[56] James Redford, "Jesus Is an Anarchist, by James Redford -- anti-state.com." Anti-State.com - Index. N.p., 19 Dec. 2001. Web. 4 Jan. 2012. <http://www.anti-state.com/redford/redford4.html>.

Even the Apostle Paul disobeyed the government and led by example. When Paul was known as Saul, he went out looking to persecute those who followed the teachings of Jesus. On the road to Damascus, Saul is said to have had a vision of Jesus. After this encounter, Saul converted and became known as Paul. Saul went from being a man who worked for the religious governmental authority to rebelling against them. He also demonstrated this when he fled Damascus as well, for the Jews were coming to arrest and execute Paul, but he escaped.[57]

Paul, who was once friendly to the needs of the government now had become an outlaw and despised governmental authority. Paul understood that the only true government is the government of the self. He demonstrated this right up to his death, like Stephen before and many more after.[58]

Now, as to not get off track, I felt that it was important to address some of the issues concerning the Apostle Paul and government. More will come, but we shall briefly continue discussing taxes.

Some will argue that Paul was for paying taxes to government, and to back up their argument, they will use Romans 13:6-7:

> For because of this you also pay taxes, for
> they are God's ministers attending
> continually to this very thing. Render

---

[57] Acts 9:1-31.
[58] Acts 7: 56-60.

therefore to all their due: taxes to whom taxes are due, customs to whom customs, fear to whom fear, honor to whom honor.[59]

On the surface, it appears that Paul supports taxes and customs. Paul makes it quite clear using rhetorical misdirection. Paul is not saying that you have to pay anyone unless you choose to, but what he is saying is that no one, especially the governmental authorities, has the right to tax or make you pay customs. Paul further explains this in the next passages:

Owe no one anything except to love one another, for he who loves another has fulfilled the law. For the commandments, "You shall not commit adultery," "You shall not murder," "You shall not steal," "You shall not bear false witness," "You shall not covet," and if there is any other commandment, are all summed up in this saying, namely, "You shall love your neighbor as yourself." Love does no harm to a neighbor; therefore love is the fulfillment of the law.[60]

Love conquers all and does not tax or coerce individuals as the government, for the government forces you to love the

---

[59] Romans 13:6-7.

[60] Romans 13:8–10.

state through fear and extortion. It's one thing to be patriotic to your government, but it is more important to be patriotic to liberty, which no government can provide or define. To fulfill God's laws is to strip off the chains of authority set up by mortal men and to love one another as God loves us. But some will mention the passage found in Titus 3:1, which states, "Remind them to be subject to rulers and authorities, to obey, to be ready for every good work."[61] In this passage, Paul is not suggesting that we submit to mortal governments that are in error, but rather those recognized by God. But those recognized by God would not be in a position to rule as one would think, for both Paul and Jesus preached the "Law" and opposed the worship of the state. The only higher authority recognized by God would be his son Jesus Christ, for he is the last "Judge" and Paul makes this quite clear.

> Dare any of you, having a matter against another, go to law before the unrighteous, and not before the saints? Do you not know that the saints will judge the world? And if the world will be judged by you, are you unworthy to judge the smallest matters? Do you not know that we shall judge angels? How much more, things that pertain to this life? If then you have judgments concerning things pertaining to this life, do you appoint those who are least esteemed by the church

---

[61] Titus 3:1

to judge? I say this to your shame. Is it so, that there is not a wise man among you, not even one, who will be able to judge between his brethren? But brother goes to law against brother, and that before unbelievers! Now therefore, it is already an utter failure for you that you go to law against one another. Why do you not rather accept wrong? Why do you not rather let yourselves be cheated? No, you yourselves do wrong and cheat, and you do these things to your brethren![62]

Paul is straightforward and clear in his message. God is the only authority: no mortal government has the right to judge, and even Jesus mentions this as well in Mark 10:42-45:

You know that those who are considered rulers over the Gentiles lord it over them, and their great ones exercise authority over them. Yet it shall not be so among you; but whoever desires to become great among you shall be your servant. And whoever of you desires to be first shall be slave of all. For even the Son of Man did not come to be

---

[62] 1 Corinthians 6:1–8.

served, but to serve, and to give His life a
ransom for many.[63]

The statement made by Jesus is simple and that is we are
not supposed to be or act as rulers. The word rulers in
Greek is *ar'-kho*[64] and Jesus makes it clear that you are not
suppose to rule over others, but rather that you be an *an-
ar'-kho* or "anarchist." The second message in this passage
is that mankind should live for one another. No, not in a
forced collectivist sense, but rather that we help one
another build a better society through voluntarism, by
praising the achievements of the individual, by building
on those achievements, for we are free and the Law of God
provides that very liberty for us to prosper.

You may look to a man and call him your leader,
your monarch, your ruler. In essence, God is the authority
for he created liberty; God was born free!

The Apostle Peter on Government and Taxes

The Apostle Peter is used at times to show support
for the role of government, as if the government's role was
a divine and necessary evil that we should obey and fear,
for God wills it. Of course, this is not true and why would
Peter wish to support or accept a government when his

---

[63] Mark 10:42–45. See also Matthew 18:4; 20:25–28; Mark 9:35; Luke
22:25, 26.
[64] James Strong, *Strong's Exhaustive Concordance of the Bible*
(Peabody, MA: Hendrickson Publications, 2004), 1610.

teacher Jesus, hated the very notion of government. The passages used to support the role of government are 1 Peter 2:13–18:

> Therefore submit yourselves to every ordinance of man for the Lord's sake, whether to the king as supreme, or to governors, as to those who are sent by him for the punishment of evildoers and for the praise of those who do good. For this is the will of God, that by doing good you may put to silence the ignorance of foolish men—as free, yet not using liberty as a cloak for vice, but as bondservants of God. Honor all people. Love the brotherhood. Fear God. Honor the king. Servants, be submissive to your masters with all fear, not only to the good and gentle, but also to the harsh.[65]

To think that Peter believed that one should submit to the government and pay taxes would be in error. Peter and the apostles were outlaws, fugitives, and rebel rousers in the eyes of the Jewish authorities. What we often forget is that the Sadducees arrested Peter and the apostles for preaching the gospel of Jesus.

---

[65] 1 Peter 2:13–18.

And when they had brought them, they set them before the council. And the high priest asked them, saying, "Did we not strictly command you not to teach in this name? And look, you have filled Jerusalem with your doctrine, and intend to bring this Man's blood on us!" But Peter and the other apostles answered and said: "We ought to obey God rather than men. The God of our fathers raised up Jesus whom you murdered by hanging on a tree. Him God has exalted to His right hand to be Prince and Savior, to give repentance to Israel and forgiveness of sins. And we are His witnesses to these things, and so also is the Holy Spirit whom God has given to those who obey Him."[66]

Peter is clear in his belief that one should obey God and not men. Even Jesus Christ said:

Jesus said to him, "'You shall love the LORD your God with all your heart, with all your soul, and with all your mind.' This is the first and great commandment. And the second is like it: 'You shall love your neighbor as yourself.' On these two

---

[66] Acts 5:27–32.

commandments hang all the Law and the Prophets."[67]

The message is simple. Treat others the way you would want to be treated. Love and respect trumps government authority for government hates love and hates liberty. Government is cold and void, while love on the other hand builds relationships and allows for individual progress, mortal authority only kills by consuming liberty in order to fulfill its evil needs. The apostles understand, risking their lives in order to spread the message of love and liberty. But in order to spread that very message the apostles had to cover up their message by writing and making statements in the form of rhetorical misdirection. For had they been blunt all the time they surely would have been dead and so would many others who followed the teachings of Jesus Christ.

Tithing and Taxes in Summary

Taxes and tithing are one in the same, but with a catch. When the state taxes you, you have no choice but to pay or face prison. Therefore, you are no more different from a slave. Your earnings are not entirely yours, for even though you may earn a paycheck, the state will take a

---

[67] Matthew 22:37-40. (For more of taxes read the excellent article "Jesus Is an Anarchist, by James Redford at http://www.anti-state.com/redford/redford4.html>.

certain amount from your earnings. However, if the state can take a certain amount of your pay, what makes you think the rest is truly yours?

Tithing is very much the same, but with a twist. Tithing in the Old Testament was voluntary up until the time of kings. Afterwards, the tithe became a tax to fund the armies and to pay the king's salary. Tithing, initially, was paid to the Levites, but God also wanted those to give, if they could, to the poor and needy, but it was not mandatory.

In the New Testament, Jesus of Nazareth condemns taxes. Jesus hated taxes, and government for that matter, and so did the apostles, as Peter and Paul mention this in their own personal writings. Government, along with taxes, was the evil that prohibited people from making progress in their own lives. Jesus and the apostles understood that to have or support a government was to support theft of both money and liberty.

Tithing in the New Testament was voluntary, as it was in the days of the Old Testament before the time of kings, but even better. In the New Testament, tithing was not about giving to support a Levitical institution. Rather, it cut the institution out and reflected it back on the individual, but it was not mandatory. If we were to tithe as Jesus did, notice the difference. Giving 10% went beyond money, it was about giving 10% of your time to help the sick get better, caring for widows and strangers, helping the poor and needy, teaching those seeking knowledge and wisdom. Love and understanding does much more and does not always require money to do so. Tithing is about giving a small amount of your time, or all of your time if one wishes to do so, so long as it helps to ease pain and suffering and promotes the individual to strive and to pay it forward. To do as Jesus did is not about self-sacrificing, but rather building a better world for the individual through the works of love and caring. No government can do a better job than the individual and Jesus and the apostles understood this. If you want to progress towards a better future, then break the shackles of government and let freedom be your guide.

Chapter 6

WAR

War can be a conflict between two people, two or more tribes, but traditionally between two nations. War for the most part is evil, but there can be a just war so long as it is a just defense.

When it comes to war in the Bible, most people think about King David. Many look to David as a sign of strength and passion. David was a great poet and musician and even a great warrior. David was indeed a warrior-poet. David is a man whom many can look up to and be inspired, but, unfortunately, many are inspired by David's military prowess. There is no doubt that David was a great politician and military strategist. Out of all the gifts David had, his ability to wage war is the one on which most people tend to focus. David's greatest gift was his love of poetry and the ability to heal a person through music and song. Unfortunately, that trait does not resonate with most people of faith and unfortunately, David sought power and glory rather than love alone.

David was indeed a "man of war"[68] but he loved war so much that it displeased God.[69] Thus, the temple in which David hoped to build to honor God went instead to

---

[68] 1 Samuel 16:18.
[69] 1 Chronicles 28:3. See also 1 Chronicles 22:8.

his son, Solomon.[70] I assume David was heartbroken by God's decision, but I also assume David understood that God hates war and the Prophet Isaiah mentions this clearly:

> He shall judge between the nations,
> And rebuke many people;
> They shall beat their swords into plowshares,
> And their spears into pruning hooks;
> Nation shall not lift up sword against nation,
> Neither shall they learn war anymore.[71]

God through Isaiah makes it clear that war shall go away for it has no place in the presence of God. Before this will occur there still will be war and we have to ask ourselves, what is a just war?

Unfortunately, today, the concept of a just war has become rather frightening and abused. Since 1945, the United States has been in the business of war making through propaganda. This started with the "Red Scare" during the Cold War, in which the U.S. made an obligation to stop the spread of communism, starting with the Korean War and later Vietnam. After the fall of the Soviet Union, the U.S. was the lone power and king maker in the world. When 9/11 happened, the U.S now had a purpose to fight again, for now we have a new threat and that threat was terrorism. The U.S. declared war on terrorism but along

---

[70] 1 Chronicles 22:9-10.
[71] Isaiah 2:4.

the way decided to expand the war into areas that were not a threat to the country, justifying it by saying that we were fighting all in the name of freedom. This is dangerous, for the U.S. not only took the war to others, but also declared war on the home front.

Therefore, what is a just war according to God? Does God approve of a preemptive strike upon those who have not attacked us? Does God approve of the state who secretly meddles in affairs of other nations? Does God approve that a nation has a right to march in and dictate what the other nation shall do? Does God approve if we meddle indirectly and decide who is king and who is not? The answer to all these questions is no!

The Root Cause of War

The root cause of war, according to the Bible, is sin. The first known war between mankind is found in the book of Genesis:

> [b]ut He did not respect Cain and his offering. And Cain was very angry, and his countenance fell. So the LORD said to Cain, "Why are you angry? And why has your countenance fallen? If you do well, will you not be accepted? And if you do not do well, sin lies at the door. And its desire is for you, but you should rule over it." Now Cain talked with Abel his brother; and it came to

pass, when they were in the field, that Cain rose up against Abel his brother and killed him.[72]

As mentioned earlier, war is not subject to nations alone. Cain was angry that his gift was not accepted, but Abel's gift was; Cain, therefore, orchestrated a premeditative strike on Abel, which resulted in the world's first murder. As mentioned earlier, Cain was the world's first statist and did what the state normally does and that is to declare war.

Jesus also laid down the root cause of war when he stated, "For out of the heart proceed evil thoughts, murders, adulteries, fornications, thefts, false witness, blasphemies."[73] Everyone commits sin, but the state sins continuously and, unfortunately, affects those under its umbrella. Yes, you could make the argument that the people are the body of the state, but this is not true. The state is an extension of a few who desire nothing more than power, and in seeking that power, will trample over the individual to achieve that very goal, which is to dominate through sin (lawlessness).

"Where do wars and fights come from among you? Do they not come from your desires for pleasure that war in your members? You lust and do not have. You

---

[72] Genesis 4:5-8.
[73] Matthew 15:19. See also Mark 7:21-23, Romans 3:10-18.

murder and covet and cannot obtain. You fight and war. Yet you do not have because you do not ask."[74]

James and the apostles, like Jesus, hated war for they understood that war is an extension of the state, an extension of one or a few men's desires to destroy the many through war and taxation. Therefore, the root cause of war is sin and sin is lawlessness, for without law no war needs justification by the few who rule over the many.

Does God Hate War?

There are those who will say God is a warmonger, drunk with blood, a tyrant, and carless. This is far from the truth, for God hates war! "For He does not afflict willingly, Nor grieve the children of men."[75] God does not take pleasure in war; nor, does he grieve for the sake of grieving due to the choices men make. God knows the heart of man and the choice a person makes is his and his alone. God's only hope is that the person, or those who that person afflicts, will rise up against the sin orchestrated against those being afflicted. The point is simple, profit from the experience to know what not to do or to allow so that can never be done to you.

---

[74] James 4:1-2.
[75] Lamentations 3:33.

In the book of Ezekiel, God states, "Say to them: 'As I live,' says the Lord GOD, 'I have no pleasure in the death of the wicked, but that the wicked turn from his way and live. Turn, turn from your evil ways! For why should you die, O house of Israel?'[76] God takes no pleasure in watching the wicked fall, but rather questions why people look to evil instead of good for their answers. Why continue the same immoral policy, both foreign and domestic, which Israel did, for it only causes strife within your borders and with those who are your neighbors? If your policy is sin, expect visitation by those like you.

King David wrote two interesting anti-war passages in which he states, "Rebuke the company of spearmen, the multitude of the bulls, with the calves of the people, till every one submits himself with pieces of silver: scatter you the people that delight in war."[77] An interesting statement coming from a "man of war" himself, but true nonetheless. War has no place among liberty minded people and especially God. "He makes wars cease to the end of the earth; He breaks the bow and cuts the spear in two; He burns the chariot in the fire."[78]

God hates war and hates the state system, for the state creates the wars in order to gain a profit, not only from the conquered but also from their own citizens. God does not approve of the state, nor did he like the idea of the Israelites wanting to be like other nations in which they

---

[76] Ezekiel 33: 11.
[77] Psalm 68:30.
[78] Psalm 46:9.

have a king and standing army to call their own. God knew that it was a matter of time until Israel decided to expand beyond its inherited borders and into the lands, which it owned not. God also understood the repercussions of this expansion by King David. To go on the offensive is to create enemies both home and abroad. After King Solomon died, Israel would suffer from this external internal strife in which the kingdom divided into two. The Northern Kingdom of Israel suffered first due to wars in the past that had not been forgotten and intermingling with nations who were hostile to them, like Assyria. The same would happen later on to the Kingdom of Judah, as well.

A Just War

All war is evil, but God does approve of self-defense. There is a good book titled *War: Four Christian Views*, written by Robert G. Clouse, which demonstrates what a just and defensible war is.

1. Just cause. All aggression is condemned; only defensive war is legitimate.

2. Just intention. The only legitimate intention is to secure a just peace for all involved. Neither revenge or conquest or economic gain or ideological supremacy is justified.

3. Last resort. War may only be entered upon when all negotiations and compromise have been tried and failed.

4. Formal declaration. Since the use of military force is the prerogative of governments, not of private individuals, a state of war must be officially declared by the highest authorities.

5. Limited objectives. If the purpose is peace, then unconditional surrender or the destruction of a nation's economic or political institutions is an unwarranted objective.

6. Proportionate means. The weaponry and the force used should be limited to what is needed to repel the aggression and deter future attacks, that is to say, to secure a just peace. Total or unlimited war is ruled out.

7. Noncombatant immunity. Since war is an official act of government, only those who are officially agents of government may fight, and individuals not actively contributing to the conflict (including POW's and casualties as well as civilian nonparticipants) should be immune from attack.[79]

---

[79] Robert G. Clouse, and Herman Arthur Hoyt, *War: 4 Christian views* (Winona Lake, IN: BMH Books, 1991), 120-121.

Seven principles in which to fight by, but my only disagreement is the idea of government leading the charge into battle, for God is not favorable of governments. But since we have a government, it would be nice if these rules were enforced. These seven principles can be applied to a stateless society, as well, just as it was before and during the time of Judges. These seven rules are in correlation with Deuteronomy 20:1-14, 19-20.

1. "When you go out to battle against your enemies, and see horses and chariots and people more numerous than you, do not be afraid of them; for the LORD your God is with you, who brought you up from the land of Egypt.

2. So it shall be, when you are on the verge of battle, that the priest shall approach and speak to the people.

3. And he shall say to them, 'Hear, O Israel: Today you are on the verge of battle with your enemies. Do not let your heart faint, do not be afraid, and do not tremble or be terrified because of them;

4. for the LORD your God is He who goes with you, to fight for you against your enemies, to save you.'

5. "Then the officers shall speak to the people, saying: 'What man is there who has built a new house and

has not dedicated it? Let him go and return to his house, lest he die in the battle and another man dedicate it.

6. Also what man is there who has planted a vineyard and has not eaten of it? Let him go and return to his house, lest he die in the battle and another man eat of it.

7. And what man is there who is betrothed to a woman and has not married her? Let him go and return to his house, lest he die in the battle and another man marry her.'

8. "The officers shall speak further to the people, and say, 'What man is there who is fearful and fainthearted? Let him go and return to his house, lest the heart of his brethren faint[a] like his heart.'

9. And so it shall be, when the officers have finished speaking to the people, that they shall make captains of the armies to lead the people.

10. "When you go near a city to fight against it, then proclaim an offer of peace to it.

11. And it shall be that if they accept your offer of peace, and open to you, then all the people who are

found in it shall be placed under tribute to you, and serve you.

12. Now if the city will not make peace with you, but war against you, then you shall besiege it.

13. And when the LORD your God delivers it into your hands, you shall strike every male in it with the edge of the sword.

14. But the women, the little ones, the livestock, and all that is in the city, all its spoil, you shall plunder for yourself; and you shall eat the enemies' plunder which the LORD your God gives you.

The rules of war 1-9 demonstrate the holiness of life, for life is precious. But when you look closely at rules 1-9, notice that no one is forced to fight. This tells us that the Israelites voluntarily assembled to fight and could withdraw anytime they wanted. Rules 10-14 highlight the need for peace between two warring parties. Verse 10 is necessary before any action is taken so that the enemy can reconsider. If the enemy asks for peace, tribute will be given to the Israelite volunteers for they came a long way leaving their farms behind and sacrificing precious time. The farmer, now turned defender, is a valuable resource to his family. If he dies, much is lost, as in labor, productivity, and profit, but if he lives, his time was lost due to the actions of the enemy. Therefore, he, like many others who journey far to defend their property, is reimbursed by the enemy due to lost productivity. It may sound silly, but when the husbands, and possibly his sons, leave to defend their property, like so many others, the work that could have been accomplished now falls on the family members who remain behind.

If the enemy decides to fight it out, the Israelites, like any other people, would fight to the death, as indicated in verse 14. Both sides fight a defensible battle, the aggressor behind his walls and the victim trying to tear down the walls. Many will be maimed and die of their wounds or be permanently handicapped by the ensuing struggle. Thus, the family back home loses loved ones and their labor. Once the city is taken, the people live, except for the males involved in the fight or so it seems. In other words, if you can voluntarily leave the assembled army, men could voluntarily refrain from killing the surviving enemy forces or even taking booty, for Deuteronomy 20:8 speaks of the "fainthearted" that are allowed to go home.

Another fascinating aspect in Deuteronomy 20 is verses 19-20. God forbids damage to the landscape, as in what we would term today as a "scorched earth policy."

> When you besiege a city for a long time, while making war against it to take it, you shall not destroy its trees by wielding an ax against them; if you can eat of them, do not cut them down to use in the siege, for the tree of the field is man's food. Only the trees

which you know are not trees for food you
may destroy and cut down, to build
siegeworks against the city that makes war
with you, until it is subdued.[80]

Not only is life precious but so is the fuel that sustains life
for both combatant and non-combatant alike. It also shows
that God was an environmentalist, unlike the many
neighbors around the Hebrew people who practiced a
scorched earth policy, such as the Egyptians, Assyrians,
Hittites, and Persians.[81]

A Standing or Voluntary Army?

In the world today, nations rely on a standing
military force paid for by the taxpayers. Not only do the
taxpayers pay for this standing army, they virtually have
no say in where the army goes and whom they fight. In the
Bible, before the time of kings, there was no standing
army. Rather, they had a voluntary force that assembled
during a time of upheaval but would dissolve after the
situation had been resolved.

The Israelite army came from the *beth'ab*
(Household), MISHP = mischpachah (Family, clan), and

---

[80] Deuteronomy 20: 19-20.
[81] Andrew Linklater, *The Problem of Harm in World Politics: Theoretical Investigations* (Cambridge: Cambridge University Press, 2011), 120.

thus the SHEVET = *shevet* (tribe).[82] The Israelites were a makeup of twelve tribes in a loosely based confederacy called Israel, which had no king but rather judges who were summoned by God in a time of emergency.

The Israelite forces had no permanent military leader; it was too risky, for the leader may take his position further and try to establish himself as king. The Israelites were careful and understood the implications of electing a permanent military leader. But when they elected a military leader, it was only temporary, as described in Judges 11:11.[83] In addition, the Israelites did not have a standing army for God was their protection in one respect, but the Israelites had no central form of government from which to expand as state traditionally does. Therefore, they were not concerned with empire building as were their neighbors.

When an invading army arrived at their border, the general or judge would sound a call to arms:

> [h]e blew the trumpet in the mountains of Ephraim, and the children of Israel went down with him from the mountains; and he led them. Then he said to them, "Follow me, for the LORD has delivered your enemies the Moabites into your hand." So they went down after him, seized the fords of the

---

[82] T. R. Hobbs, *A Time For War: A Study of Warfare in the Old Testament* (Wilmington, Delaware: Michael Glazier, 1989), 35.
[83] Judges 11:11.

Jordan leading to Moab, and did not allow anyone to cross over.[84]

Another example of the call to arms is mentioned in the book of Judges 6:34-35:

> But the Spirit of the LORD came upon Gideon; then he blew the trumpet, and the Abiezrites gathered behind him. And he sent messengers throughout all Manasseh, who also gathered behind him. He also sent messengers to Asher, Zebulun, and Naphtali; and they came up to meet them.[85]

Even the prophet and judge known as Samuel made a call to arms when the Philistines attacked:

> And Samuel said, "Gather all Israel to Mizpah, and I will pray to the LORD for you." So they gathered together at Mizpah, drew water, and poured it out before the LORD. And they fasted that day, and said there, "We have sinned against the LORD." And Samuel judged the children of Israel at Mizpah. Now when the Philistines heard that the children of Israel had gathered

---

[84] Judges 3:27-28.
[85] Judges 6:34-35.

together at Mizpah, the lords of the Philistines went up against Israel. And when the children of Israel heard of it, they were afraid of the Philistines So the children of Israel said to Samuel, "Do not cease to cry out to the LORD our God for us, that He may save us from the hand of the Philistines." And Samuel took a suckling lamb and offered it as a whole burnt offering to the LORD. Then Samuel cried out to the LORD for Israel, and the LORD answered him. Now as Samuel was offering up the burnt offering, the Philistines drew near to battle against Israel. But the LORD thundered with a loud thunder upon the Philistines that day, and so confused them that they were overcome before Israel. And the men of Israel went out of Mizpah and pursued the Philistines, and drove them back as far as below Beth Car.[86]

The Israelite forces involved in this fight were voluntary as well. Israel may have a general or judge looking over them during a time of battle, but the rules still apply to those who want to help in the war effort, even to those who have no stomach for it as mentioned in Deuteronomy 20:5-9. Being released from military duty due to inexperience, as in the case of Gideon and his "Valiant Three Hundred," is

---

[86] 1 Samuel 7:5-11.

another example of people coming together during crisis, and they did so voluntarily. In the book of Judges 7:1-7 it states:

> Then Jerubbaal (that is, Gideon) and all the people who were with him rose early and encamped beside the well of Harod, so that the camp of the Midianites was on the north side of them by the hill of Moreh in the valley. And the LORD said to Gideon, "The people who are with you are too many for Me to give the Midianites into their hands, lest Israel claim glory for itself against Me, saying, 'My own hand has saved me.' Now therefore, proclaim in the hearing of the people, saying, 'Whoever is fearful and afraid, let him turn and depart at once from Mount Gilead.'" And twenty-two thousand of the people returned, and ten thousand remained. But the LORD said to Gideon, "The people are still too many; bring them down to the water, and I will test them for you there. Then it will be, that of whom I say to you, 'This one shall go with you,' the same shall go with you; and of whomever I say to you, 'This one shall not go with you,' the same shall not go." So he brought the people down to the water. And the LORD said to Gideon, "Everyone who laps from

the water with his tongue, as a dog laps,
you shall set apart by himself; likewise
everyone who gets down on his knees to
drink." And the number of those who
lapped, putting their hand to their mouth,
was three hundred men; but all the rest of
the people got down on their knees to drink
water. Then the LORD said to Gideon, "By
the three hundred men who lapped I will
save you, and deliver the Midianites into
your hand. Let all the other people go,
every man to his place."[87]

Thirty-two thousand volunteers showed up, Twenty-two
thousand volunteers return home, while ten thousand
stayed. But ten thousand was far too many for the mission.
Therefore a test had to be done and the test determined
that only three hundred men were fit.

Another key aspect in this system of a volunteer
army is that the leader of the army would have to maintain
a much higher level of loyalty and respect for his men.
Unlike the modern military of today, where an enlisted
man is forbidden to fraternize with the officer for fear of
punishment. This promotes semi-loyalty at best in respect
to both the officer and the enlisted men under the officer's
guidance. To find real loyalty, one must look to the lower
ranking enlisted men, for they live together and are free to
socialize with one another. Thus, the enlisted men are loyal

---

[87] Judges 7:1-7.

to one another due to the system that forbids interaction on a social scale with their superiors. Therefore, they may take orders from above and respect the rank, but their true loyalty is with each other.

The Bible clearly demonstrates this loyalty and friendship to one another. To follow an officer who doesn't give a damn is costly, but to fight for an officer who acts humanly, like Gideon, is rewarding for he will receive love and respect for because he will bleed with you and understand that your life is just a precious as his.

War in Summary

Therefore, to have a standing army is to pay for wars through money and blood. Your sons and daughters will be at the whim of state; you have no say for the state trumps liberty and in war liberty is first to go. Even Gideon understood this for the Israelites wanted to elect him as their king, but Gideon said, "I will not rule over you, nor shall my son rule over you; the Lord shall rule over you."[88] If you choose to have a volunteer army, which can come and go as they please, it is not a statist army by definition, but rather men and women fighting for the same cause and that is for the defense of liberty, which is loyalty, and most importantly, shows love for one another.

The Bible clearly demonstrates God's hatred for war, for men with power can sway as easily as the wind.

---

[88] Judges 8:23.

God hated the idea of a king presiding over Israel or any nation for that matter. God hates the useless shedding of blood for there is no need of war. But if you must war, make it quick and show mercy, for not only do you suffer but your enemies suffer as well, and so do the families not involved in the conflict. Show love, for love is the essence of God and love will end conflict.

Chapter 7

Is God a Monarchist or Anarchist?

And I heard another voice from heaven saying, "Come out of her, my people, lest you share in her sins, and lest you receive of her plagues." —Revelation 18:4

This is the mother and father of all questions! Many say that when God returns, or when Jesus returns, or when they both return together, they will establish a monarchy. If God establishes a monarchy, it is a rule of one, for *mon* = one, *archy* = rule or authority. Some say this is a metaphor, but Christian Apologist had to do something in order to change the nature of Christianity so it doesn't look polytheistic due to the concept of the Trinity, which is the Father, Son, and Holy Ghost.[89] Eventually the church leaders came up with the concept that God shared his rule, with God being the head of course, but even this is problematic for they see God as a theocratic monarchy and fail to understand that God is not in favor of governments in any form.

Christians and Jews believe that a monarchy will be established, but this goes against God's nature as we have read. Others will say that when God and Jesus return to

---

[89] Kevin Giles, *Jesus and the Father: Modern Evangelicals Reinvent the Doctrine of the Trinity* (Grand Rapids, Mich.: Zondervan, 2006), 177.

earth they will establish a theocracy. This I agree with but only partially. Yes, in a sense, God's rule on earth would be a theocracy but no, he will not rule as a dictator demanding his will be done. In other words, to tell someone what they are going to do is to dictate the everyday aspect of their life. If God were to do this, he would violate his own belief in free will.

When we turn to the stories found in the Bible, we find they do not promote or suggest that God is a dictator looking to enslave man but rather the opposite. The stories we read in the Bible are about responsibility, self-governing, and ownership in which the Ten Commandments are the principles supporting that philosophy. If you think God is looking to punish and enslave mankind for all its wicked deeds, then what was the point of instituting free moral agency, free will, or even liberty?

God will establish his place here on earth at some point, but government will be non-existent. Instead, God will establish a non-government. The only state to exist will be that of the individual through the act of self-rule. This would create an environment of persuasion and cooperation, for to force anyone to accept anything against their will would be ungodly. Think of the examples God has demonstrated in the Bible already. In the Garden of Eden, God seems to visit from time-to-time. Adam and Eve go about their business until they sin. God did not kill them, but rather punished and banished them from the garden. Once Adam and Eve were in the wild they still lived free and made choices like anyone else, and still God was there to help them if needed. No hell, no purgatory, no fire to be thrown into. Another example would be Cain after he murdered Able, for Cain's punishment was banishment from the community and isolation. Cain was not killed for his actions, but rather Cain lived with the memory of his sin until he died and that was punishment enough in God's eyes.

Even Abraham, Isaac, and Jacob all sinned, but their failure cost each one of them, but again, no death, rather guilt turned to understanding and they lived free and with God's guidance. The same goes for the time of Judges, for all men did what they saw fit in their own eyes, but when a king was requested all of this changed for the worse.

Therefore, God is not a king but rather a just judge serving the people and dealing with the day-to-day issues that materialize. God and Jesus have no interest in ruling people as we see how the state rules its people today, through burdensome unjust laws and lawless regulations, which impede the individual from truly living a free life.

Conclusion

Put not your trust in princes, nor in the son of man, in whom there is no help. —Psalm 146:3

My question goes out to the Christian, the Jew, or anyone for that matter, and that question is why do you support the state? If God never intended for humanity to have a system in which one or a few rule over the many, then why do you support such a system when that system was born out of iniquity? Why do you support all the evils that come with the state when God and his son Jesus, clearly are anti-state, anti-tax, and anti-war? God is pro-peace, pro-property, and pro-prosperity. God advocates cooperation and persuasion and in no way wants humanity to hurt, harm, or coerce others who have different beliefs or different lifestyles.

In no way, am I advocating for the creation of a theocratic government for that would be wrong and would go against God's own principles. You, like me, are our own governments, our own markets; thus, the individual is a state and market unto himself or herself.

Many of you may like the Constitution of the U.S. You have to remember, though, that the Constitution is nothing more than a piece of paper written by men. Yes, it says many great things, but in essence, it is just a piece of paper, a document that can be changed and overlooked, as we witness today and makes the concept of freedom rather cheap. The Constitution guarantees nothing; whereas, God guarantees everything for you are born free and no social contract has the right to determine how much liberty you shall have. But God guarantees total liberty for you are responsible for your own actions.

> And (Jesus) seeing the multitudes, he went up into a mountain: and when he was set, his disciples came unto him:
>
> And he opened his mouth, and taught them, saying,
>
> Blessed are the poor in spirit: for theirs is the kingdom of heaven.
>
> Blessed are they that mourn: for they shall be comforted.
>
> Blessed are the meek: for they shall inherit the earth.
>
> Blessed are they which do hunger and thirst after righteousness: for they shall be filled.
>
> Blessed are the merciful: for they shall obtain mercy.

Blessed are the pure in heart: for they shall see God.

Blessed are the peacemakers: for they shall be called the children of God.

Blessed are they which are persecuted for righteousness' sake: for theirs is the kingdom of heaven.

Blessed are ye, when men shall revile you, and persecute you, and shall say all manner of evil against you falsely, for my sake. Rejoice, and be exceeding glad: for great is your reward in heaven: for so persecuted they the prophets which were before you.

Ye are the salt of the earth: but if the salt have lost his savour, wherewith shall it be salted? it is thenceforth good for nothing, but to be cast out, and to be trodden under foot of men.

Ye are the light of the world. A city that is set on an hill cannot be hid. Neither do men light a candle, and put it under a bushel, but on a candlestick; and it giveth light unto all that are in the house. Let your light so shine before men, that they may see your good works, and glorify your Father which is in heaven.[90]

[90] Matthew 5:1-16

Bibliography

Clouse, Robert G., and Herman Arthur Hoyt. *War: 4 Christian Views*. Winona Lake, IN: BMH Books, 1991.

Giles, Kevin. *Jesus and the Father: Modern Evangelicals Reinvent the Doctrine of the Trinity*. Grand Rapids, Mich: Zondervan, 2006.

Hobbs, T. R. *A Time For War: A Study of Warfare in the Old Testament* . Wilmington, Delaware: Michael Glazier, 1989.

Linklater, Andrew. *The Problem of Harm in World Politics: Theoretical Investigations*. Cambridge: Cambridge University Press, 2011.

Olive, J. Michael, and Donald C. Stone. ""Exclusive Interview With Murray Rothbard." ." *The New Banner: A Fortnightly Libertarian Journal 1, no. 3*, 1972: 1-4.

Redford, James. - anti-state.com." Anti-State.com - Index. N.p., 19 Dec. 2001. Web. 4 Jan. 2012. <http://www.anti-state.com/redford/redford4.html>. ""Jesus Is an Anarchist." *anti-state.com*. December 19, 2001. http://www.anti-state.com/redford/redford4.html (accessed January 4, 2012).

Strong, James. *Strong's Exhaustive Concordance of the Bible*. Peabody, MA: Hendrickson Publications, 2004.

von Mises, Ludwig. *Omnipotent Government*. Grove City, PA: Libertarian Press, Inc., 1985.

Wiersbe, Warren W. *The Wiersbe Bible Commentary. 2nd ed.* Colorado Springs: David C Cook, 2007.